·····In·Time·of·Need·····

War

by Sean Connolly

FRANKLIN WATTS
LONDON • SYDNEY

An Appleseed Editions book

First published in 2004 by Franklin Watts
96 Leonard Street, London, EC2A 4XD

Franklin Watts Australia
45–51 Huntley Street, Alexandria, NSW 2015

© 2004 Appleseed Editions

Created by Appleseed Editions Ltd,
Well House, Friars Hill, Guestling, East Sussex, TN35 4ET

Designed by Ian Butterworth

ISBN 0 7496 5710 3

A CIP catalogue for this book is available from the British Library.

Photographs by:
AP/Wide World Photos, Corbis (AFP, Adrian Arbib, Bettmann,
Jonathan Blair, BLEIBTREU J/CORBIS SYGMA, Hulton-Deutsch
Collection, Wolfgang Kaehler, Kelly-Mooney Photography, Jacques
Langevin, Wally McNamee, Medford Historical Society Collection,
PAVLOVSKY JACQUES/CORBIS SYGMA, Reuters, David Turnley)

Printed in the USA

Contents

What Is War?

Everyone has had an argument at one time or another. Usually the argument is nothing more than that – an exchange of angry words. And usually the people arguing calm down and reach some sort of agreement, perhaps guided by parents or friends. Sometimes, however, the argument can turn into a violent fight, in which one or both people lose their tempers and hit each other.

Groups of people, and even countries, can also behave this way. Countries have differences of opinion with other countries, which they normally try to settle sensibly and peacefully. But every so often, these differences seem to grow, and neither side is willing to back down. And like the people who use their fists in an argument, they may turn to violence instead of talking. If one country chooses violence, other countries may feel they do not have a

Above: When people disagree, they sometimes fight. On a global scale, this can lead to war. Left: An illustration depicting the 30 Years War in 17th century Europe.

4

choice, as when Great Britain declared war on Germany in World War II (1939–45) in order to stop the **Nazis** from taking over Europe.

Wars can last many years and involve many people. In the 1600s, for example, most countries in western Europe were involved in a war that lasted 30 years. More recently, in the 20th century, millions of people fought each other in two **world wars**. Not only did these wars involve many countries, but new weapons, using advances in the fields of chemistry, biology and physics, as well as new technology such as computers, made the fighting even more intense than in earlier wars. These advances have continued, and today's weapons are deadlier than any seen before.

Below: British soldiers in Iraq use a computer to operate their command post and improve the accuracy of rounds fired at the enemy.

THE SOCCER WAR

Two neighbouring Central American countries, El Salvador and Honduras, had many disagreements throughout the 1960s. When their soccer teams played each other in a series of World Cup games in June 1969, the sports rivalry was the last straw. On July 14, 1969, war broke out between them. The war lasted only four days, but it left 3,000 dead, 6,000 wounded, and caused £30 million worth of damage. There were far deeper reasons for fighting than simply a dispute over soccer, but people still refer to the conflict as the 'soccer war'.

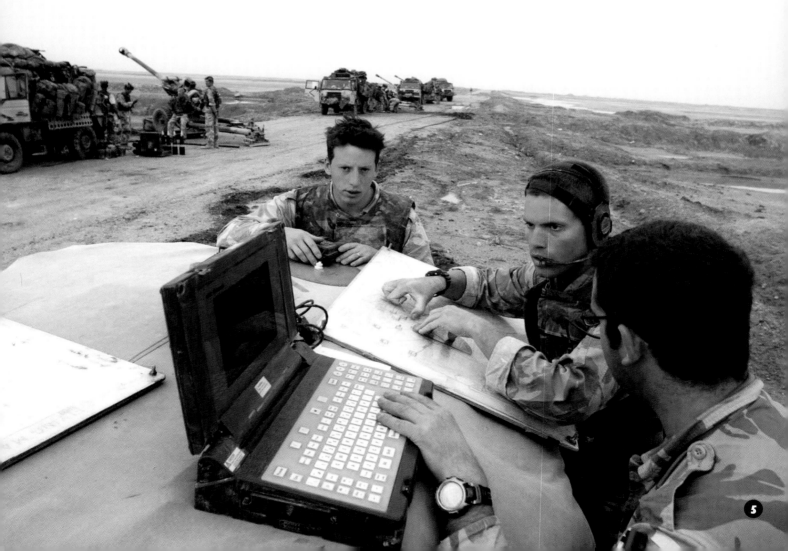

A long-running dispute turned into fierce fighting in 1999 in East Timor, part of an island that lies north of Australia. Indonesia had invaded East Timor in 1975. Most of the islanders wanted to be independent, but Indonesia used its army to maintain control. One islander, who preferred to keep his name secret, described how a neighbour had heard firing and went out of his house to see who it was. Soldiers chased him and shot him dead. 'His wife and children were also chased and almost killed. His wife ran into the hospital. They hid in a medicine cabinet. They climbed inside, and then other friends hid them there. Later they were able to get out and escape.' In the space of a few minutes, a whole family's life had changed.

'As a result of the explosion of the bomb at 8:15, almost the entire city was destroyed at a single blow.'
Father John A. Siemes, an eyewitness describing the effects of the atomic bomb dropped on Hiroshima, Japan, at the end of World War II

'War is hell.'
US General William Tecumseh Sherman recalling the US Civil War

The Human Cost

The results of war can be devastating. During the six years of World War II, more than 20 million soldiers died. As many as 40 million people not directly involved with the fighting lost their lives. Still more people were left homeless after the war.

Of course, not every war is as wide-ranging as a world war. Some conflicts take place within one country, either as a **civil war** or as a **revolution**. Sometimes a group of people will single out a city or even just one building to create confusion and fear. The destruction of New York's World Trade Center, or Twin Towers, on September 11, 2001, was a dramatic example of such **terrorism**.

No matter how large or small, violent conflicts carry a painful cost to human life. Many people die or lose loved ones. Many more lose their homes and their ability to earn a living. Innocent people become victims, just as they would in a tornado, earthquake or flood. They can only hope for peace and a chance to rebuild their lives.

Below: A view of Hiroshima, Japan, shortly after it was struck by an atomic bomb. Opposite: The US dropped an atomic bomb on Nagasaki, Japan, three days after dropping one on Hiroshima. Japan surrendered five days later to end World War II.

Battles
of Ideas

Many wars begin out of a dispute about land. Germany invaded Poland at the start of World War II in order to get more 'living space' for its own people. Iraq invaded its neighbour Kuwait in 1990 in order to gain control of land that was rich in oil. Wars such as these continue the tradition that began thousands of years ago, as nations developed armies and weapons to attack their neighbours.

But **conquest** is not the only reason that nations go to war. Many of the most savage wars have been fought over ideas. These ideas often deal with some of life's basic issues, such as which type of government is best or how people should worship.

Above: A Kuwaiti military helicopter flies overhead as Iraqi prisoners cross a stream during Operation Desert Storm. Left: Troops patrol the border between Pakistan and India, where disputes over land keep tensions high between the two countries.

8

HEARTS AND MINDS

Some experts on conflict say that wars are won and lost in people's 'hearts and minds'. Persuading people that it is right to risk their lives by fighting – winning their 'hearts' – is an important part of winning a war. Convincing them that the war can actually be won – winning people's 'minds' – is another important part.

Sometimes governments will use PROPAGANDA to convince people. This information might be aimed at the government's own people, in order to assure them that they are all working together for a good cause. Posters during World War II told people that 'Careless talk costs lives'. That advice made people cautious about accidentally giving away important information to strangers who might be spies. Propaganda can also be aimed at people on the other side. In 2002, for example, US forces dropped leaflets in Afghanistan urging the Afghan people to join the effort against the ruling Taliban party and terrorists in hiding.

Right: A female soldier fights for Vietnam during the fall of Saigon in 1975. Win or lose, soldiers must be willing to risk their lives for their country when they go to war.

THE KILLING FIELDS

The southeast Asian country of Cambodia suffered while its neighbour Vietnam went through a fierce civil war for more than 20 years. But as Vietnam's war ended in 1975, Cambodia's real tragedy was just beginning. A group of extreme communists known as the Khmer Rouge seized power in Cambodia. Everything in the country had to change to fit their way of thinking. The year 1975 became known as 'Year Zero' because it was the beginning of Cambodia's new way of life. People whom the Khmer Rouge did not trust were sent away from their families to work long hours in rice fields. These fields were like open-air prisons, with armed guards ready to shoot anyone who complained or did not work hard enough. Between 1.5 and 2 million people died of starvation, disease, or EXECUTION in the two years that the Khmer Rouge controlled Cambodia.

Below: Union (Northern) soldiers capture Confederate (Southern) fortifications in Petersburg, Virginia, near the end of the US Civil War in 1865.

Civil War

Clashes about ideas have also led people in the same country to fight against each other. Such a conflict is called a civil war. England had a civil war in the 1640s over who should have more power, the king or the elected members of parliament. The American Civil War of 1861 to 1865 was also fought over some big ideas. The southern states wanted the right to govern themselves. They wanted to form a new country that would guarantee the right of landowners to own slaves. The northern states – most of which had made slavery illegal – wanted to keep the southern states as part of the US. People were ready to die for their ideas in each of these civil wars. Even families were divided. Brothers fought against brothers, and fathers against sons.

Civil wars still take place today. Sierra Leone, a West African country, was torn apart by a civil war in the 1990s. More than 100,000 people died – a huge number in such a small country – before a **treaty** was signed in 1999. The nearby country of Ivory Coast endured four months of civil war in 2002 after rebels overthrew the government.

Left: A rebel soldier in Bouake, Ivory Coast, during the country's 2002 civil war.

THE COLD WAR

World War II ended in 1945, but for nearly 50 years afterwards the world went through a tense period known as the Cold War. At its heart was a conflict between two types of government. Each side was led by a mighty SUPERPOWER. One of these superpowers was the SOVIET UNION, which believed that COMMUNISM was the best way to rule people. Facing the Soviet Union and its ALLIES was a group of countries led by the United States, which believed that DEMOCRACY was the best form of government. Each superpower had NUCLEAR WEAPONS aimed at its rival, and they continued to build more until the United States and the Soviet Union each had enough to destroy each other – and the entire world. People worried that any argument between the two superpowers would trigger a deadly war. Luckily, such a war never took place. By 1991, most countries had chosen to get rid of their communist governments, and the Cold War ended.

Soviet missiles were often paraded through the streets of Moscow, Russia, during the early years of the Cold War.

Freedom Fighters?

Most American schoolchildren learn about the 'shots heard round the world' in 1775. The battles in Lexington and Concord, Massachusetts, triggered the fighting in the American Revolution. A year later, the 13 British **colonies** declared themselves a new, independent country – the United States of America. In 1783, Great Britain signed a treaty in which it agreed that it no longer had any control over the United States.

The story is familiar, and Americans are right to be proud of the 'Founding Fathers' who helped give birth to the new country. What might be harder to understand is that – at least from the British point of view – the Americans did not 'play by the rules'. The British army, like other European armies, believed that battles should be

Above: Guerilla fighters from a rebel group in India. Left: During the American Revolution, colonists did not conform to the techniques of traditional warfare, but instead caught the British soldiers off-guard with guerrilla tactics.

fought according to certain traditions. In particular, armies lined up opposite each other and either marched forward or shot at the enemy from where they stood. The Americans often hid behind trees or hills, picking off British soldiers as if they were hunting deer or rabbits.

A New Type of Fighting

The type of fighting used by the colonists during the American Revolution is called **guerrilla warfare**. The name comes from a Spanish word meaning 'little war'. Guerrilla wars usually have few old-style battles, with both armies lined up against each other. Instead, soldiers hide and wait for opportunities to make quick attacks before disappearing again into hiding.

Since the American Revolution, many other wars have been fought with similar methods. Most Americans would describe the colonists as the 'good guys,' because they were fighting for a cause now believed to be right. In other words, they are viewed as freedom fighters. But what about the many wars and struggles that have been fought in the same way since?

'Kill off all the people, including small children and old people – those who live in Dili are all considered to be pro-independence.'
Part of a letter written by an army commander during the fighting in East Timor

'Many a good lad had nothing to cover him from his hips to his toes, save his blanket.'
One of George Washington's officers describing the harsh conditions for American colonists fighting the British during the winter of 1779

Below: Guerilla fighters at a makeshift camp along the Thai-Burma border in 2000.

The saying, 'One man's terrorist is another man's freedom fighter' sums up the difficulty of deciding whether a particular struggle is right or wrong.

Big Questions

Wars that do not obey the 'rules' are harder to control and also harder to prevent. Guerrilla wars frequently pit a group of inexperienced soldiers against a much larger army. The army usually has more soldiers and weapons, and it controls most roads, train lines, airports and other lines of communication. The only way that the guerrillas can hope to overturn such an advantage is to strike wherever and whenever they feel they can damage the larger army. In the case of the American colonists, that meant hiding behind trees or in swamps and forests.

Other groups fighting against powerful countries or armies go much further. They believe that attacking places and people that have nothing to do with armies or war – targetting civilians – will force the enemy to back down. No one can be sure where, when, or even how they will strike. Because their main weapon is fear, these people are called terrorists. They are sometimes willing to give up their own lives to make an attack succeed. That was true of the terrorists who carried out the September 11 attack on the Twin Towers. These 'suicide' attacks are especially difficult to prevent.

Above: The World Trade Center in New York after the attacks of September 11, 2001.

ACTING FOR PEACE

We consider the Twin Towers attack to be evil and wrong, just as Americans believe that the American Revolution was right. But much of the world's fighting is far less clear-cut. Sometimes it seems that both sides – or neither side – of a conflict can be seen as partly right. The world watches helplessly as thousands or even millions of people die in the confusion. This sort of tangled conflict struck the African countries of Somalia, Sierra Leone, Liberia and Ivory Coast as well as parts of India, Pakistan, and many other countries in recent years. The only hope in these wars is that both sides can agree to some sort of outside help to end the fighting. An outside peace-keeping force can prevent small incidents from building up into more fierce fighting. Then both sides can concentrate on finding a way of achieving a lasting peace.

Above: Israeli police and paramedics work at the scene of a suicide bombing in Jerusalem in 2002, where six civilians were killed and at least 84 wounded.
Opposite: Suicide bombers often pick urban targets such as crowded buses or busy streets to make their attack.

Caught in the
Middle

Even the most normal everyday things in life – going to school, playing, harvesting crops, and travelling – become almost impossible during a war. There is danger everywhere. Everyone suffers, including people who do not agree with the reasons for going to war. The most serious dangers, of course, come from weapons. Millions of people died during World War II because their villages or cities were attacked or bombed. Other people died of starvation because their farms were burned or trampled by soldiers and equipment. Smaller wars leave a similar trail of death and damage, which ordinary people must face each day.

Above: The Red Cross provides medical assistance to refugees in war-torn places such as Kosovo. Left: Jewish refugees await their release from a displaced persons camp after World War II.

EMERGENCY RELIEF

A number of international organisations back up the front-line work of the Red Cross and Red Crescent on the battlefield. Medicins Sans Frontieres (Doctors Without Borders) sends medical teams to help the sick and wounded. Relief teams are often needed long after the fighting has stopped. Disease and hunger become problems in places where fighting has disrupted normal sanitary and medical routines and food supplies. Such organisations as Oxfam and Save the Children lead efforts to help war-torn countries regain their ability to look after themselves.

OUTSIDE HELP

Countries going to war are supposed to obey certain rules that have been agreed upon by the world community. These rules, known as the Geneva Conventions (after the Swiss city in which they were agreed upon), are intended to keep the fighting limited to armed soldiers on either side. In other words, the rules are aimed at protecting civilians as much as possible.

They also require fair treatment of PRISONERS OF WAR. Special organisations that are accepted as NEUTRAL by both sides, such as the International Red Cross and Red Crescent, are given protected status in the war zone by the Geneva Conventions. These organisations send people to check on conditions in battle zones and send food and medical supplies to prisoners.

Left: Rwandan refugees, made homeless by civil war, line up for Red Cross grain handouts.

17

A GIRL'S VIEW OF GETTYSBURG

Tillie Pierce was born in 1848 and lived all her life in Gettysburg, Pennsylvania, where an important battle of the American Civil War was fought in 1863. Like other families in Gettysburg, the Pierces could not stop the Southern troops from LOOTING their homes to stock up on food, clothing and other supplies before the battle. Here she describes the actions of the enemy troops:

'Whatever suited them they took. They did, however, make a formal demand of the town authorities, for a large supply of flour, meat, groceries, shoes, hats, and (doubtless, not least in their estimations) 10 barrels of whiskey; or, [instead] of this five thousand dollars.'

'On Christmas day we were to receive Red Cross parcels – one to every five prisoners. Imagine the excitement and eagerness we felt when Christmas day actually arrived! Here was this parcel containing lots of good things – tea, chocolate, canned meats, canned milk, butter, jam – all ready for eating.'
British soldier John Airey describing his time as a prisoner of war during World War II

Without a Home

The troubles do not end when soldiers lay down their weapons and come to a peace agreement. Millions of people lose their homes because of war. Homes may be destroyed in the fighting, or they may be taken away by a new government that has seized power. Many people become **refugees**, forced to leave their villages and even their countries so that they can find somewhere more welcoming and peaceful to live. The United Nations High Commission for Refugees is the leading international organisation looking after people's needs and helping them face their new troubles in the wake of war. Some people do not believe that the incoming refugees are genuinely in danger in their homeland and do not think they should be allowed to stay. This can make it hard for the refugees to settle into new jobs and schools.

> There are more than 20 million refugees in the world today. Nearly a third of them live in south-west Asia (mainly Iran and Pakistan), North Africa, and the Middle East.

HIDDEN KILLERS

Wars can continue to kill innocent people long after the fighting has officially ended. Many of these deaths come from land mines, hidden bombs buried underground. Armies lay these mines in places where enemy soldiers are likely to walk. The mines explode when someone walks over them, killing or seriously injuring the person. Unfortunately, the mines often remain unexploded after fighting has stopped. Local people on their way to school or work can trigger an explosion, with deadly results. Mines continue to kill innocent people in many countries, especially Afghanistan, Cambodia, Iraq, Iran, Nicaragua, Angola and Mozambique. The International Committee to Ban Landmines is the leading organisation trying to stop their use. Its campaigning efforts, coupled with its first aid relief to land mine victims, earned it the Nobel Peace Prize in 1997.

'I was excited by the peace. I and my family hoped to return to peace. We wanted no memories of war. However, my brother, on the long walk home, stepped on a land mine and lost his foot. What have I done to deserve this? They told me we had peace.'

Alice Simbane, a Mozambican refugee speaking in December 1992

Above and left: Tired refugees make their way back to Germany from the Czech territory after World War II.

I WAS A CHILD SOLDIER

Paska Achieng Otto was just 14 years old when she was forced to join armed rebels in Uganda. She soon found herself in command of about 1,000 rebel troops. But Paska wanted to escape the death and destruction. Around Christmas in 1987, she and a small force of rebels staggered across the border into Kenya, where Kenyan troops put them in prison. Two years later, the United Nations and the Canadian government helped Paska move to Canada, where she has lived ever since.

Child Soldiers

For children, who may not even understand why a war is being fought, life in a war zone is terrifying. They go to sleep not knowing if they will wake up. Although this way of life is unsettling for young people, it could be even worse: they could be among the soldiers fighting.

Above: In developing nations such as Uganda, young children may be forced to serve as soldiers when conflict arises.

Children fight alongside adults in many parts of the world. They go to war for many reasons, but very rarely because they wanted to join the fighting. Often the only place where they can get regular meals or a bed is with the same soldiers who might have just destroyed their village. Other child soldiers may come from a town or region that has been captured. Invading troops sometimes turn their prisoners – including children – into fellow soldiers. But no matter how they have received their weapons, these children are expected to kill – and risk being killed – just like the other soldiers.

A group of more than 500 organisations is urging countries to approve a new international treaty that would ban armies from using children as soldiers. The United Nations (UN), an organisation of 189 countries, approved the treaty in May 2000, but so far no more than a handful of countries have signed it.

The UN's work for peace does not end when the fighting has stopped. Many people, especially children, remain afraid and uncomfortable living in a country that has just witnessed terrible fighting. After several wars that raged as Yugoslavia broke up into different countries in the early 1990s, the United Nations Children's Fund (UNICEF) moved in to help frightened children. It published the words and pictures of more than 50 children in its book *I Dream of Peace: Images of War by Children of Former Yugoslavia*. The book gave children a chance to write and draw things they found hard to say. Maida, a 12-year-old girl, wrote 'War is the saddest word that flows from my quivering lips. It is a wicked bird that never comes to rest.'

> **M**ore than half a million children (younger than 18) are serving as soldiers in more than 87 nations. Some of these child soldiers are as young as seven.

'The shooting started – boom! People were dropping like fish. My major thing was just to try to get the [wounded] people out.'
Paska Achieng Otto remembering her first battle as a child soldier in Uganda

Left: The United Nations is working to stop countries from using child soldiers, but many developing countries are hesitant to make the commitment.

Wars of the Future

In the early 1990s, the communist governments of Russia and its East European neighbours collapsed. Their new governments did not consider the United States to be an enemy. They also promised to work together for peace in other parts of the world. Most people were relieved at this news, since it meant that there was far less chance of another world war taking place in the future.

Unfortunately, the same decade saw old wars continuing and new ones developing in many parts of the world. The powerful Middle Eastern country of Iraq invaded its neighbour Kuwait in 1990. The United Nations responded by sending soldiers to drive Iraq's soldiers back from Kuwait. UN forces employed many new weapons that had computers to find targets more easily and accurately, speeding up the end of the war and sparing many civilians. International cooperation and the effectiveness of these new weapons made many people hope that the world was entering a fairer, more peaceful age.

Left: After Iraq's 1990 invasion of Kuwait, the United Nations responded by sending a multinational force to the region that included this convoy of British tanks.

New Enemies, New Weapons

Perhaps it was too early to predict a new age of peace based on international agreement. Iraq once more dominated the news in 2002, as its government seemed to hamper UN efforts to check on its weapons. The world would not accept a build-up of Iraq's weapons because of fears that Iraq might repeat its attack on Kuwait, or attack some other country. US, British, and Australian forces formed another **coalition** in 2003, which defeated Iraq's government in an effort to establish a more peaceful government in that country.

Countries can unite to form a powerful force against actions such as Iraq's. But they can do far less to prevent conflict and warfare within countries. For example, a number of fierce civil wars raged through Europe, Africa and Asia while UN forces were bringing peace to Kuwait in 1991.

Another deadly problem – international terrorism – seemed to grow stronger at the same time. The September 11 attack on New York's Twin Towers was the most obvious example of this terror in action. But it continues in Asia, in Israel and neighbouring countries, in parts of Europe – in fact, almost everywhere. And new fears have arisen that terrorists might be able to buy or produce terrible new weapons such as **nerve gas** and even atomic bombs. One of the most troubling things about terrorism is that terrorist organizers – unlike governments – disregard international agreements about how wars should be fought.

In the days following the September 11, 2001, attack, President George W. Bush announced a war on terrorism that aimed to hit at the heart of the terrorist problem. Countries that protected terrorists would themselves become targets in this war. In 2002, a US-led coalition was sent to Afghanistan, where many of the September 11 terrorists had lived and trained. The coalition defeated the Afghan government troops and forced the terrorists to surrender or flee the country.

'This is unbelievable – perhaps another low level tourist ride; perhaps he came low to avoid another aircraft; perhaps . . . perhaps . . . as we watch the plane pass the Empire State Building and then diminish in size until . . . until . . . poof, a large ball of flame emerges from the twin tower . . . all at once everyone is screaming.'
A construction worker's view from a skyscraper of the September 11 terrorist attack on New York

Above: The terrorist attack on New York's World Trade Center on September 11, 2001, prompted the US to announce a war against terrorism.

War Crimes

Over the years, groups of countries such as the United Nations have tried to make rules about how wars are fought. The rules try to protect civilians and prisoners of war. Sometimes military leaders or ordinary soldiers deliberately break these rules and act with great cruelty. They destroy villages, round up and shoot innocent people, and force people to work as if they were slaves. All of these actions are examples of war crimes, behaviour that the world believes is unacceptable and should be punished, even in times of war.

Above: The entrance to the infamous German concentration camp of Auschwitz-Birkenau in Poland. Left: A crematorium in a concentration camp discovered after World War II contains evidence of the horrible atrocities committed by the Nazis.

Special Trials

After the fighting has ended, international organisations try to find those who are accused of war crimes. They try to find out the truth and then punish the guilty. All of this takes place in special **trials**. The most famous war trials took place in the German city of Nuremburg just after World War II ended. Many German wartime leaders were tried and convicted of terrible crimes, in particular the killing of millions of Jews and other people. More recent war trials have looked into crimes committed during the wars fought in the former Yugoslavia in the 1990s.

Below: Hermann Goering was one of 24 Nazi leaders tried for war crimes in trials held in Nuremberg, Germany, from October 18, 1945 to October 1, 1946.

TARGETTING A NATION

Countries or groups involved in wars usually attempt to defeat the countries or groups they consider to be the enemy. Sometimes, however, a country or its army will go much further by trying to wipe out all of the people in the country or ethnic group they view as their enemy. This type of organised mass murder is known as genocide, from the Latin words meaning 'killing a people.'

Genocide is one of the worst crimes that anyone can imagine. During World War II, Nazi rulers believed that Jewish people were evil. They rounded up millions of Jews and sent them to brutal camps. In what later became known as the Holocaust, as many as six million Jewish people were deliberately killed.

Organized mass murder continues to be a terrible reality. From 1981 to 1983, the army of the Central American country of Guatemala killed thousands of local Indians. Soon after Bosnia declared independence from Yugoslavia in 1992, Croats and Bosnian Muslims became the targets of Bosnian Serbs. As many as 250,000 people were killed, and 2.3 million people became homeless. In 1994, about 500,000 out of 800,000 Tutsi (a people living in the East African country of Rwanda) were killed by soldiers of the Hutu people who ruled the country.

The Search for Peace

Few people enjoy the death and destruction caused by war. It would be wonderful if someone could simply say 'Stop fighting', and warring armies would return to their bases. But if we think that a war is often like a children's argument – only far more serious – then we can see how hard it can be to return to peace. Unless one side in a war defeats the other outright, the two sides need outside help (like the teacher or friend in a children's argument) to stop the fighting. Otherwise, small incidents – possibly unrelated to the immediate dispute – could trigger another war.

For centuries, countries have tried to resolve their differences by talking rather than fighting. Skilful people, known as diplomats, represent the countries in these discussions with neighbours and other nations. They hope to get the best deal for their own country without going to war. Sometimes diplomats from both sides can work behind the scenes to prevent or end a war.

Above: A peace flag at an antiwar protest in 1971. Left: Members of the 'Women's Strike for Peace' protest the Vietnam War in 1967.

Getting Together

By the 20th century, it had become clear that diplomats working one-to-one with other diplomats could not prevent every war. And with new, much more destructive weapons available, these new wars could lead to the deaths of millions of people. A group of countries joined to form the League of Nations in 1919, just one year after the bitter fighting of World War I (1914–1918) had ended. Diplomats from 63 countries met and talked together to try to stop further wars.

Sadly, the League of Nations was unable to prevent an even deadlier war, World War II. Part of the problem was that many powerful countries, including the United States, never became members of the League. Even before World War II had ended, diplomats began meeting again. They wanted to form a new, stronger group to settle countries' arguments peacefully. By late 1945, they had formed the United Nations.

'I hope world leaders involved in war create a plan to protect children before and during war. It would be even better that for the next 10 years we have less conflict in my country.'
Diana, 17, from Serbia, speaking in 2002

Below: The US involvement in the Vietnam War caused strong reactions across the country. Demonstrators often gathered to protest the war with banners, signs, songs and chants.

OTHER MEASURES

The international community has other ways to contain conflict. Regional groups such as the European Union (EU) and the Economic Community of West African States (ECOWAS) sometimes form peacekeeping missions in their own regions. Military alliances such as the North Atlantic Treaty Organisation (NATO) use military power to stop any conflict that threatens their members. International organisations try to restrict the military power of countries that have acted aggressively. Weapons inspectors were sent to limit the amount of weapons held by Germany after World War I and Iraq after the Persian Gulf War of 1991.

Sanctions, such as restrictions on buying and selling goods, are sometimes used to force a country to behave more peacefully, but it is hard to enforce such a programme over a long period, and such measures often affect the country's poorest citizens rather than its leaders. Perhaps the best way to build a more peaceful world is to change the way people think. For example, children from both sides of the Northern Ireland and Middle East conflicts have spent vacations together in summer camps where they can learn how much they have in common.

The UN has grown throughout its history, and now has 189 member-countries. These countries must promise to be 'peace-loving', which echoes the goals of the UN's founding members. The UN has formed many different organisations to solve problems with education, food, health and housing around the world, but working towards and protecting peace remain its most important goals.

The United Nations has no army of its own and cannot send troops to settle conflicts that arise around the world. It relies on member countries to supply troops and equipment for **peacekeeping** operations. These troops fly the UN flag on their vehicles and wear the distinctive blue helmet of UN peacekeepers. Since the first UN peacekeeping mission in the Middle East in 1948, the 'blue helmets' have been involved in more than 50 missions around the world. Some of these, such as the mission to the Dominican Republic from 1965 to 1966, have helped bring about peace. Others have been less successful, but they have still reduced the fighting.

Above: Sometimes celebrities try to use their fame to encourage peace. Singer John Lennon and his wife, Yoko Ono, were vocal opponents of the Vietnam War. Opposite: The mother of a fallen soldier protests the Vietnam War in 1965.

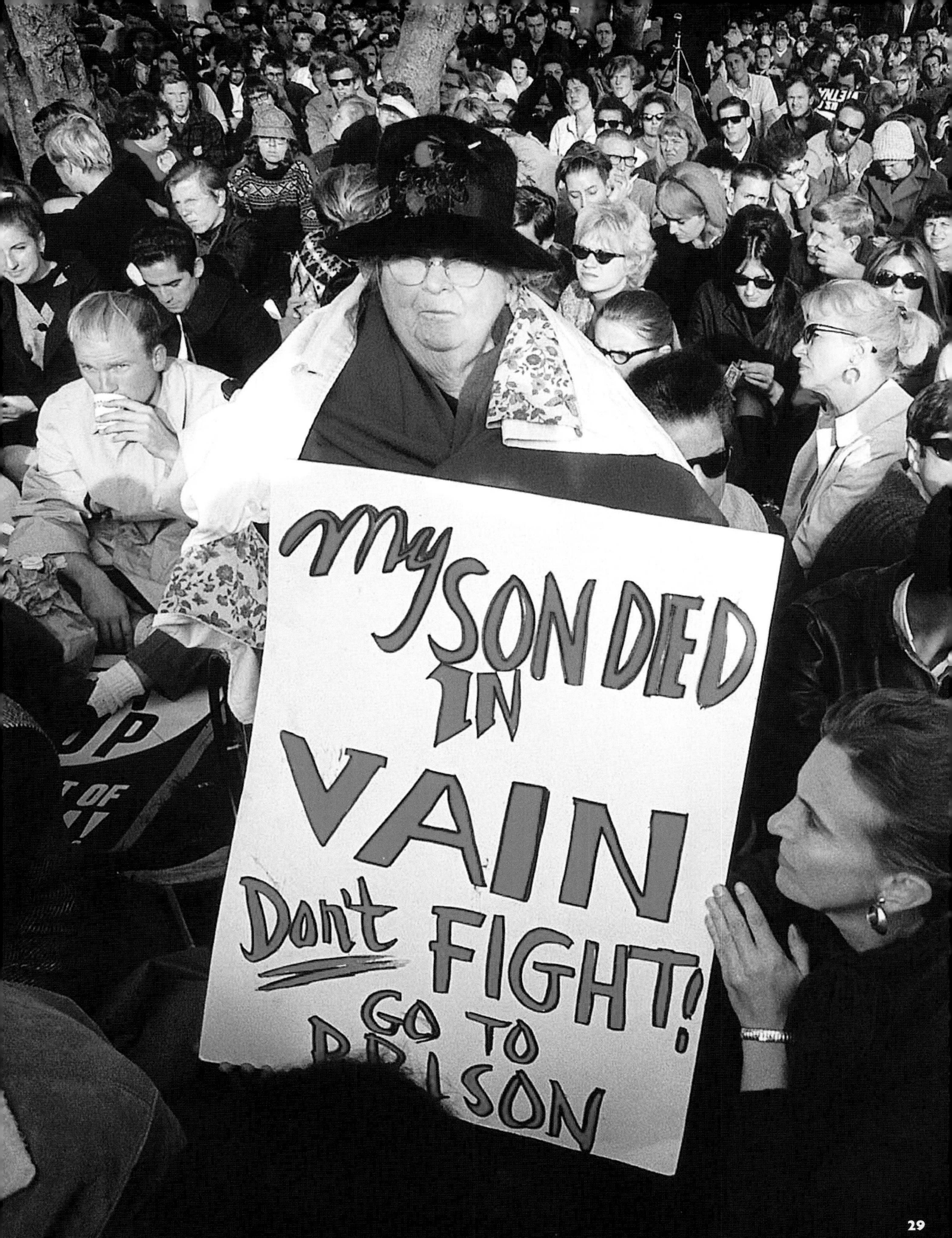
My SON DIED
IN
VAIN
Don't FIGHT!
GO TO

Glossary

allies countries that help each other during a war

atomic bomb a powerful bomb that releases the power of atoms, tiny bits of matter; atomic bombs are also called nuclear weapons

civil war a war fought within a country between two or more groups from that country

coalition a group of countries that share a military goal

colonies settlements that are geographically separated from, but governed by, another country

communism a way of ruling a country in which all property is owned by the government

conquest conquering or taking control of another land or group of people

democracy a form of government in which the people vote for those who will lead them and laws are passed by elected officials

execution the deliberate killing of someone by a government

guerrilla warfare a type of warfare that involves stealth attacks rather than open battles

looting stealing from stores or houses when there is no police force to protect people's property

Nazis members of the political party that ruled Germany during World War II (1939–45)

nerve gas poisonous gas used as a weapon

neutral not taking sides

nuclear weapons see atomic bomb

peacekeeping the work done by soldiers sent by the United Nations or another organisation to keep peace in a war zone

prisoners of war soldiers captured by the enemy during a war

propaganda information used to scare an enemy or to boost the spirits of the home country during a war

rebels people fighting against their own government

refugees people who have lost their homes because of a disaster such as war

revolution the use of violence to replace one government with another

sanctions restrictions placed on a country by other countries in response to a violation of international law

Soviet Union a communist country made up of Russia and 14 other nations that was formed in 1917 and dismantled in 1991

superpower a country that has enough weapons and military power to defeat most other countries

terrorism a type of fighting that targets ordinary people rather than soldiers and uses fear to win battles

treaty an agreement between two or more countries, usually to end a war

trials investigations in a court of law to determine whether someone is guilty of a crime

world wars wars involving many countries in different parts of the world

Further Information

Books

What's at Issue? War & Conflict,
  by Sean Connolly.
  Oxford: Heinemann Library, 2001.

Hostage to War: A True Story,
  by Tatiana Vasileva.
  London: Collins Educational, 1999.

Parvana's Journey,
  by Deborah Ellis.
  Oxford: Oxford University Press, 2002.

Web sites

Medicins Sans Frontieres
www.msf.org

International Committee of the Red Cross and Red
Crescent (ICRC)
www.icrc.org

United Nations
www.UN.org

Campaign for Nuclear Disarmament (CND)
www.cnduk.org